Survival Guide:

TOP Secrets Of Finding Edible Wild Plants And Mushrooms

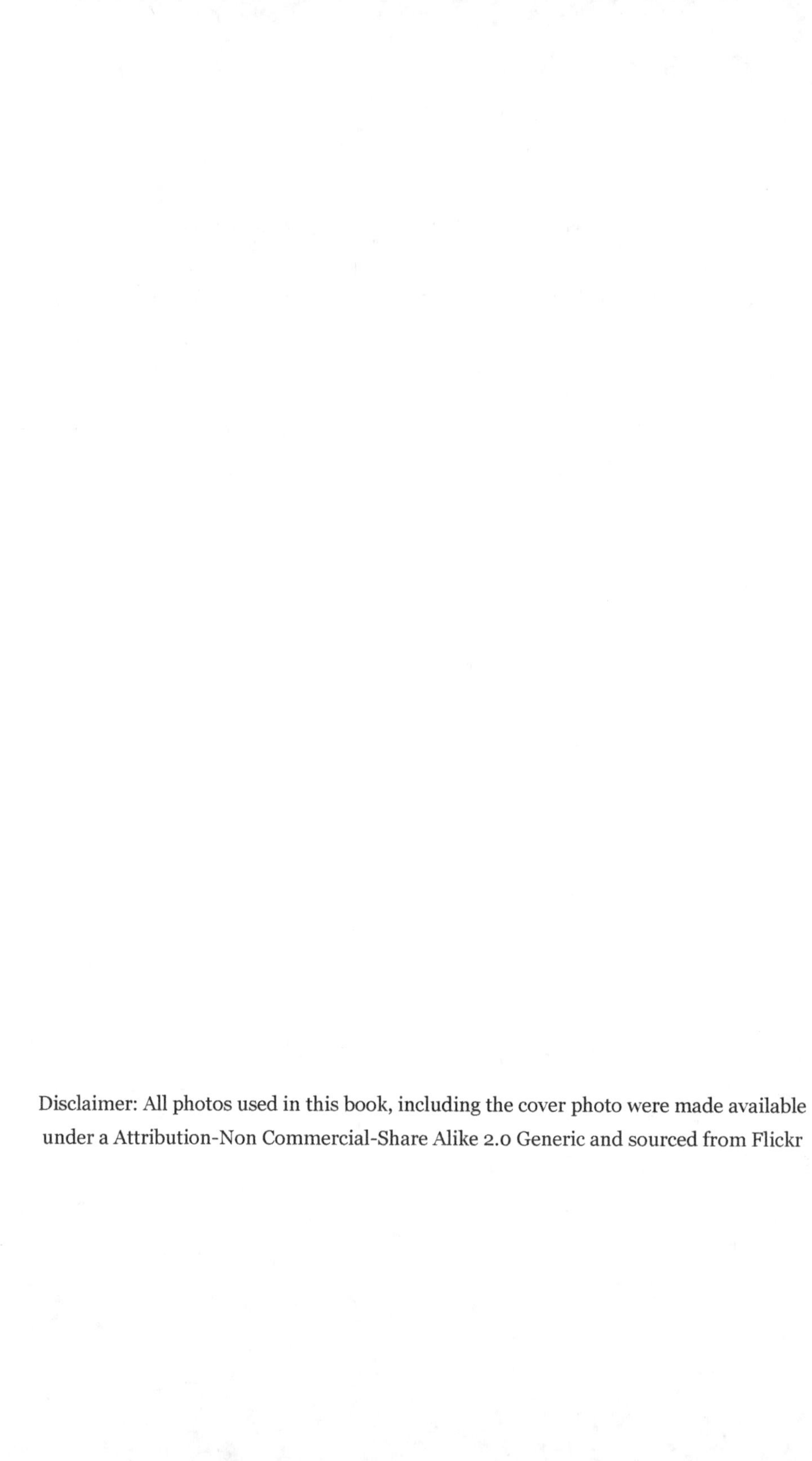

Table of content:

Introduction: Getting Back to Our Foraging Roots

In the modern world, gathering our fruits, veggies, mushrooms, and meat, is done by driving ourselves to the grocery store and browsing the aisles from there. Few today would consider going out into the open terrain to gather our food from the wild. Yet, the best way to know what you're getting, and that it is of true quality, is quite literally, to *get it yourself*. Because whether we realize it or not, all of that heavily processed food they hand to us at the super market has lost half of its value by the time it makes its way to the store shelves.

They mark the food up with a shelf life, but in reality, the life was already half gone by the time it hit the store shelf in the first place. Don't trust the shelf life of grocery store foods, and don't be dependent on them for your survival. Instead learn to get back to your roots and forge your own path by foraging in the forest! As you progress through this book you will truly learn how it is that you can get back to your foraging roots! Feel free to take notes, and experiment along the way!

Chapter 1: Best Foods to Forage in the Spring and Summer

When you think about it Spring and Summer are the times of year that the planet really comes to life. All kinds of plant and animal life come out of their winter hibernation and make their presence known. Having that said, the Spring and Summer months are the prime time to forage. Here are some of the best finds of the season.

Hawthorn

Right at the outset of Spring, the white flower petals of the Hawthorn plant begin to emerge. The sight is an unmistakable sign that the warmer months of Spring are on the horizon. These eye-catching flowers are not only good to look at however, they are also very good to eat. The roughage of this plant makes for a great salad. And if you wait just a little while longer as Spring begins to turn into summer the berries that form on this plant can be collected and turned into a tasty, all-natural jelly for your toast! And if all that jelly makes your thirsty, the leaves of the Hawthorn plant can be boiled up into an excellent tea to drink. Hawthorne is the foraged food that just keeps right on giving!

<u>Stinging Nettle</u>

Growing as a wild root all over the Springtime landscape the leave from this plant are rich in phosphorous, iron, silicon, and calcium. Think of it as a vitamin from Mother Nature! This herb comes straight from the ground, and right into your bloodstream, to inject with the kid of sustenance that only nature can provide. You will find this hearty herb growing in patches that are about 4 or 5 inches off the ground. Stinging Nettle is best picked out of the ground right when it first sprouts up. Many who are iron deficient have greatly benefit by adding a little Stinging nettle to their diet, due to its high level of natural iron deposits.

Burdock Root and Stalks

Have you ever walked through a wooded area and left surprised to find sticky little burrs stuck to your boots (or Nike high tops, or however it is that you roll) and the bottom of your jeans? These little hangers-on come from the burdock stalks that you must have undoubtedly brushed against during your trek through the forest. And while the burrs themselves are not really edible the stalks they came from as well as the very roots of the plant, are very good foods to forage.

The roots are best picked in early Spring, and the stalks are at their best in early Summer. The stalks themselves serve as a great kind of veggie, almost like an artichoke or some similar green vegetable, and work quite well in either salads or in stir fry. The roots are very much edible as well, but are actually most popularly used in teas. Burdock root tea is one of my personal favorites, and if you haven't tried it, I suggest giving it a go yourself sometime soon.

<u>**_Strawberries_**</u>

Just as easily as you buy these fruits from the grocery store you can find them growing in the wild. They usually start popping up in overgrown fields right around late June. You may have even seen these guys sprouting up through the cracks of city sidewalks. The only real difference between wildly growing strawberries and the store-bought kind is that they are smaller—thus as you walked by that sidewalk crack of strawberries you probably didn't pay much heed to them, because they were most likely on the tiny side. Many who come across these bright red, small berries believe that they are poisonous, but they are note. They are just as healthy as the larger store-bought variety, and they taste just as good too! Gather these guys up wherever you see them!

Violets

This foraged food is no shrinking violet! By May you will find these flowers growing proud and strong. They typically stay in season from May all the way to August, and can be found in the woods and even in your own backyard. Like many plants, Violets shoot off spore, which once taken by the wind can spread to just about anywhere. So, it is for this reason that you can see these flowers sprouting up in such diverse locations. Violets are completely edible. You can eat everything on this plant, from the tip of the flower all the way to its root. So don't be shy, and don't shrink form foraging this Violet!

<u>**Blueberries**</u>

Blueberries like Strawberries are at their best during the Summer season. They tend to grow the most up north in North America and Northern Europe. Canada especially seems to have more than adequate conditions to produce plenty of these berries in the wild. These berries tend to grow in big sporadic patches across fields and meadows, but they have also been seen growing out of such less than idyllic situations such as sidewalk cracks and even abandoned buildings. At any rate—they are good to eat, so if you see them—pick them up!

Chapter 2: The Fall and Wintertime Harvest

The Fall and Winter months are like the closing chapters of the year. But although this natural last chapter and epilogue serves to signal an ending, these final seasons of the year still have plenty of beginnings of their own. There are many unique foods that stubbornly grow in Fall and defy all odds by sprouting right in the middle of the coldest Winter. Here are just a few examples of them.

Acorns

No, they're not just for squirrels. Acorns have been safely foraged and consumed by human beings for tens of thousands of years. There are a lot of things you can do with fresh acorns, you can even ground them down into a kind of acorn-flour and make pancakes out of them if you like! Having that said, this is a wildlife staple not to be missed from your routine. If you live up north these guys fall out of trees every fall and can be collected right off of the ground.

Just make sure that you rinse them off before attempting to eat them, for sanitary purposes as well as to wash off the bitter and sour residue that the exterior of most acorns come covered with. Don't be alarmed this bitterness is not a sign of poison, it's just not a pleasant flavor for most. But once this residue is rinsed off you can boil the acorns, or grind them into powder and make quite a bit of use of this wild staple food you have foraged.

<u>*Mustard Seeds*</u>

For those of you that like a little flair and spice, as it turns out nature provides us with alternatives just as nice! Mustard seeds are a fairly solid crop during the months of Fall, and can be harvested any time between early September all the way until mid-November. Mustard seed crops typically grow out in open meadows with plenty of late Fall sun shining down on them. If you are looking for mustard seeds—the funny thing about it is— you will most likely smell them before you ever even lay eyes on them!

That's just how strong their mustard aroma is. It's so distinct, it works as its own calling card. But besides smell, you will notice the mustard plant through its bright yellow flowers, and heart shaped seedpod structure. Gather as much of this plant as possible during your foraging, and you can grind the seeds and make your own homemade jar of mustard! And then terrific homegrown flavor of mustard straight out of mustard seeds is not something to be missed!

Shamrocks

Are you feeling lucky? Well how about trying your luck out with some shamrocks? These readily foraged foods are iconic with their shamrock shape, and stand out just about anywhere they grow. They are also a completely nutritious food to eat either as salad based roughage or as boiled or fried greens. Shamrock's grow in batches that reach up to as much 7 inches tall. The shamrock leaves are usually the familiar bright green that most of us are used to, but sometimes has a faded caste, or pale greenish hue.

The shamrock leaf is also adorned with whitish pink flowering as well. This plant is not poisonous and can be eaten without fear. However, it must be stressed that you shouldn't *over eat* from this plant. Shamrock's are a natural source of oxalic acid, which is fine for us in most circumstances, but if you eat too much shamrock you can cause your body to accumulate too much of it. This can then lead to some rather painful and distressing results in the form of a kidney stone later on! And this is a rather *unlucky* situation to find yourself in!

Watercress

Watercress is the wilderness lettuce of the wintertime. You can find this tasty plant growing near frozen lakes and snow-covered foliage in forests and meadows. This food in its natural state is highly nutritious and entirely edible, but there is one caveat on the edibleness of watercress. Due to the fact that this plant tends to grow near lakes, rivers and streams, you are going to have to take special care to make sure that these bodies of water are far removed from any source of runoff pollution from factories.

Since President Nixon began the EPA (environmental protection agency) all the way back in the 1970's much of North America's runoff problems have been solved. But it only takes one bad actor to create a problem for the rest of us, so always make sure you know what might be in the neighboring environment of where you forage for your watercress.

Chickweed

Chickweed has been known to grow right out of snowy embankments. It's flowers stand out in harsh winter landscapes as an oasis of grace and beauty. These chickweeds are also highly edible too. Locate a patch of them where the sunlight has removed some snow. Gather up as much of these plants as you can and boil them in soups, or add them in salads. This is a true survival food that can survive the harshest of winter weather. It will be a great boon to you as well.

<u>Wintergreen</u>

As the name just might imply, this is a plant that sprouts up its green leaves right in the middle of the winter. It grows low to the ground near trees and just out of reach of the snow. The leaves have an excellent mint flavor that works out just great in coffees and teas. They also make for a good salad. This plant is prevalent throughout much of the northern regions of North America and Europe. Wintergreen is a great find for any forager.

Chapter 3: Find Edible Mushrooms and Avoid Poisonous Fungi!

Finding a patch of mushrooms is a real treat for any foraging adventure but you have to make sure that you avoid batches of mushrooms that are poisonous. Although most wild mushrooms are harmless, there are a few varieties of mushroom that are downright toxic and should be avoided at all cost. Look at this chapter as your complete foraging guide to the Fungi Kingdom.

Oyster Mushrooms

Oyster Mushrooms are a hardy variety of fungus that can be found clinging to the sides of rocks and trees even during the coldest months of the year. They are easily recognized by their oyster-like shape from which they are aptly named. These tough little mushrooms often emerge in early January right after freshly fallen snow has blanketed forest floors, with the tops of their clam-like caps poking up through the snow, as they cling to tree roots and trunks in the woods.

Giant Puffball Mushroom

Some have likened a sighting of these mushrooms as something akin to finding a mushroom shaped soccer ball laying in the woods. These mushrooms are usually about 12 inches across, but have been known to become much bigger. And the skin is usually white and completely smooth, hence, its "Giant Puffball" name. These Giant Puffball Mushrooms are attached to, and grow completely out of the ground, without the traditional mushroom stem for support.

The Puffball species of mushroom is indeed edible, but there are a few other kinds of mushrooms that mimic the appearance of the Puffball which are not ideal mushrooms at all. In order to avoid eating the wrong kind of mushroom, you need to be able to know what the Giant Puffball Mushroom looks like in the first place. The best way to know just what you are dealing with when it comes to these puffy kinds of mushrooms is to cut them open and look inside at the material.

In order for a mushroom to be a true "Puffball" it needs to be uniformly white on the inside. I call this the snowball puffball test. If it is as white as snow on the inside of the mushroom you know it is the real deal, but if you see black spots on the inside, you know that you are dealing with one of its slightly toxic cousins. These mushrooms have a similar taste to that of store bought button mushrooms and work well diced up in salads, and as a topping element such as on pizza.

<u>Yellow Chanterelles</u>

These edible mushrooms can be found growing just underneath the soil of hardwood trees such as oak and conifers. The caps of these mushrooms stand out for their yellow color, and grow to as much as 5 inches across. The caps of the mushrooms expand as they get older and tend to be wrapped up close to the stalk when the mushrooms first begin to sprout. The stems themselves tend to be fairly smooth and are white in color. These mushrooms go great in stir fry. Gather as many as you can!

Jack o' Lantern Mushrooms

These *poisonous* mushrooms are lit up, bright orange like a Jack o' Lantern, and are clustered close together right around the roots of trees. The gills of this mushroom have clearly defined edges, and easily disintegrate when handled. If you suspect you are in the presence of Jack o' Lantern Mushrooms, avoid them. If you touch them, wash your hands immediately.

Those said to have been affected by the toxins in this mushroom have experienced severe nausea, stomach cramps, and distressing diarrhea. This is definitely not my idea of a good time! Those who have been poisoned by this mushroom usually need to be administered an IV solution overnight in order to help stabilize them and rid their body of this poison. Be sure to avoid any Jack o' Lantern Mushrooms you may find.

Chicken Mushrooms

This mushroom is also sometimes called Chicken of the Woods, and is very popular among foragers and survivalists alike. These mushrooms sometimes appear as dull as the ground that they are attached to, but at other times are easily identifiable for their bright orange and yellow colorings. It is also for this reason that many novice mushroom hunters mistakenly believe that these mushrooms are poisonous.

And this is not without good reason, because much of the time when nature colors something bright red or bright orange, whether it be the leaves of a plant or the markings of a poisonous spider, it is a clear indication that the organism sporting those colors are somehow harboring harmful toxin. But in the case of these mushrooms, this couldn't be further from the truth, they are completely edible and completely nutritious. Having that said however, these mushrooms have been known to cause some mild indigestion.

But besides the rare stomach cramp, these mushrooms shouldn't cause you any problems. Furthermore, it has been suggested that it is the older mushrooms that cause this particular problem. But when they are picked early in the season, there shouldn't be any issue. These mushrooms are predominately found on the West Coast of North America. These mushrooms should be plucked from the ground while their caps are still tender, and meaty. Some say that the fleshy bulbs of the mushroom tastes like chicken, and it is for this reason that they get their name.

Chapter 4: Forever Foraging Perennials

Perennial plants are those that last over several seasons. These plants can be safely harvested and foraged all year round. Here are just a few examples of this kind of food that you can forage.

Rhubarb

Rhubarb makes for some tasty pastries, salads, and just about everything else! This plant is loaded with nutrients and flavor. You can typically find these plants growing in big patches, about 4 feet in width, with their green leaves and reddish stalks shooting up out of the ground. Pick these plants when you are sure they are ripe, and large enough to be harvested. The edible parts of this plant are actually the stalks and the roots, the leaves however are not to be eaten and should be discarded as soon as you pick the plant up out of the ground.

<u>Artichoke</u>

Growing in fields of bright sunshine, the artichoke can reach heights of as much as 8 feet. The whole plant is edible, but it is the leaf of the artichoke that is the true prize. The leafy greens of this plant are perfect for salads, stir fry, and as just plain sides of roughage at your dinner table. Artichoke roots are also of use and have been utilized to create all manner of coffees and teas.

Asparagus has seen a renaissance at the grocery store and has become one of the most popular foods in the produce aisle. But you don't have to go to the supermarket to get a good supply of this plant. Just go outside! This plant is a true perennial and can be found sprouting up in meadows with their stalks waving through the breeze. Asparagus is most prevalent in the Southwest of North America. If you know where they are don't hesitate to snatch them up. This plant is good cooked or even just consumed right out of the field.

Sweet Potatoes

Sweet Potatoes are a staple of the Fall and Winter holiday season, but this perennial plant actually grows year-round. They grow in rich soil with a lot of sunlight. They are most easily recognized by their yellow roots that come up out of the soil. If you see these sweet potato plants growing in the wild don't hesitate to pull them out by the root and save them for later!

Ground Plums

If you see these ground plums growing off the vine don't hesitate to snatch them up! These hardy plums grow year-round with the most minimal of resources. You can find them hanging tight in rough terrain such as deep forests and even on mountain sides. But wherever you find them it's a tasty treat. These plums can be cooked or even eaten raw. Ground plums are definitely a food that is worth foraging.

<u>***Broccoli***</u>

Yes, broccoli is a perennial plant and can be foraged all throughout the year. In the wild broccoli grows to a pretty good height and the heads are clearly seen sprouting up out of the plant. These plants actually grow nonstop for a few years straight making them well within the parameters of a perennial plant. The entire broccoli plan is edible, making it the perfect food to forage.

Indian Potatoes

These plant does bear some resemblance to the standard potato, but it really is nothing of the sort. This foraged food is actually fruit that grows right off the vine. These vines are huge and grow all year round to some pretty astonishing lengths. The "potatoes" that grow out of these vines are green to yellow in color. This perennial plant can be foraged and eaten without any fear. So, if you see them hanging from the vine, feel free to grab a few and take them home.

Chapter 5: Best Food Preservation Techniques

Now that you have your food foraged and stockpiled together, you will need to know some basic food preservation techniques. Here in this chapter we will discuss some of the best ways to maintain the food you have gathered.

Using Root Cellars

Root cellars have been used for hundreds of years and before we had electricity to cool down food they were the go to source for preservation of fruits and veggies. These root cellars work by utilizing the natural coolness of the Earth in order to consistently bring down the temperature of the food. Just like a refrigerator it preserves food through lowering their temperature levels. Root cellars can be dug right into the ground, sometimes even right into the side of natural rises in the Earth such as a hillside.

They can also be made by converting subterranean household structures such as basements into food storage units. In order to turn a basement into a makeshift root cellar. You just need to wall off one corner of the basement with boards of wood and then place some wooden slats down in that corner for your produce to sit on in order to avoid rot from moisture. Keep a thermometer handy in this corner so that you can effectively gauge the temperature your produce is being subjected to.

And that's about it! By doing this you can use the natural coolness of the ground to preserve all those foods that you so painstakingly foraged! Using root cellars can really pay off, so don't hesitate to employ it for yourself!

<u>*Making Use of Foraging Pits*</u>

Dug out forage pits work on the same exact premise of a root cellar. They are simply a means to utilize the coolness of the Earth in order to better preserve your produce. You can dig this whole right into your property if you like or find some other secluded spot you are allowed to dig into. Once your foraging pit has been dug out you can then add some bedding in the form of leaves or maybe even hay at the ground level of the pit. This should provide proper insulation for your foraged fruits and veggies.

Once this layer is in place you can drop all the items that you have foraged down on top of it. Next, take another layer of leaves or similar roughage and place it on top of your produce. Then finish it all up by covering the pit with a few inches of soil. The fruits of your foraging should now be stored and ready for you almost indefinitely. Making use of foraging pits can be of great benefit.

Use Food Drying Techniques

Drying out food is kind of a lost art, but we still see it pop up from time to time in the form of items such as beef jerky and the like. But it isn't just beef that can be dried out, all manner of fruits and vegetables can be easily dried and saved for later consumption as well. Raisins for example are simply dried grapes. It's amazing how many people don't realize that fact, but it's true.

In order to preserve your own foraged fruits and veggies through drying, just put the food up in a high place where the sunlight can beam down on them. That's really all you have to do, nature naturally dries out our food for us. If you want grapes just place a bucket of them up on a high structure that receives plenty of sunlight and they will dry and shrivel up into raisins in no time. Using food drying techniques to preserve foraged food can be of tremendous help.

Make use of Canning Jars

The process of canning food has been with us for quite some time, and it is a timeless and effective means of food preservation. Whatever it is that you have foraged simply place it in a glass mason jar, and fill it to the max, making sure that everything is pressed down and no air pockets are made. After you have done this place your lid on the jar and tighten it shut. Now you will need to subject the jar to high heat in order to truly pressurize it and can it.

There are whole machines and apparatuses available to do this, but really all that is required is boiling water. So, having that said, if you are out in the wild with a backpack full of mason jars. You can your food on the spot by filling them up, sealing them, and then placing the jar into the middle of a large cooking pot. Fil that pot with water and cook it over a fire. Once the jar has been submerged in boiling water for 20 to 30 minutes, consider it canned!

Conclusion: Finding Your Way Through Foraging

Some have asked why such an ancient practice such as foraging for food has become so popular as of late. But for those who know the thrill of grabbing life by the horns, and taking your own destiny into your own hands, they already know the answer. We don't forage because we have to, we forage because we want to. We thrive on the notion that we are making our own way in life, and foraging is just one expression of that independence. I hope that this book has instilled some of that same selfsame spirit in you as well! Thank you for reading!